R9/5

Simp

CW00815932

A ZEBRA BOOK
Illustrated by Elizabeth Wood

PUBLISHED BY

WALKER BOOKS

LONDON

Simple Simon met a pieman
Going to the fair;
Says Simple Simon to the pieman,
Let me taste your ware.

Says the pieman to Simple Simon,

Show me first your penny;

Says Simple Simon to the pieman,

Indeed I have not any.

Simple Simon went a-fishing,

For to catch a whale;

All the water he had got

Was in his mother's pail.

He went to try if cherries ripe

Did grow upon a thistle;

He pricked his finger very much,

Which made poor Simon whistle.

He went to catch a dickey bird,

And thought he could not fail,

Because he'd got a little salt,

To put upon its tail.

He went to ride a spotted cow,

That had a little calf;

She threw him down

upon the ground,

Which made the people laugh.

Simple Simon went a hunting,

For to catch a hare;

He rode a goat about the streets,

But couldn't find one there.

He went to eat honey,
Out of the mustard pot;
He bit his tongue until he cried,
That was all the good he got.

He went to shoot a wild duck,
But wild duck flew away;
Says Simon, I can't hit him,
Because he will not stay.

Once Simon made a great snowball,

And brought it in to roast;

He laid it down before the fire,

And soon the ball was lost.

He went to take a bird's nest,

Was built upon a bough;

A branch gave way, down Simon fell,

Into a dirty slough.

He went to slide upon the ice
Before the ice would bear;
Then he plunged in above his knees,
Which made poor Simon stare.

He went for water in a sieve,
But soon it all ran through;
And now poor Simple Simon
Bids you all adieu.